Little Pinoy Explorers'

Symbols of the PHILIPPINES

Written and illustrated by:

Mary Repollo

This book belongs to:

_____

Copyright © 2025 by Mary Repollo.

All rights reserved.

No part of this publication may be reproduced, distributed, or transmitted in any form or by any means, including photocopying, recording, or other electronic or mechanical methods, without the prior written permission of the publisher, except in the case of brief quotations embodied in critical reviews and certain other noncommercial uses permitted by copyright law. For permission requests, write to the publisher, addressed "Attention: Permissions Coordinator," at repollomary17@gmail.com.

Any facts provided in this book has been checked for accuracy from the time of publication.

Written and Illustrated by Mary Repollo

First printing edition 2025.

ISBN: 978-0-6458805-4-0

Hi! I'm Amihan.

I'm here to show you around and introduce the different symbols of the Philippines. We'll start off with the seven national symbols and the rest will be the cultural symbols that represent our Filipino roots.

Let's go!!

NATIONAL FLAG

This is the Philippine flag or "Pambansang watawat ng Pilipinas". It is a symbol of freedom, bravery, and the enduring aspirations of the Filipino people.

Its blue stripe represents peace, truth, and justice, while the red stripe symbolizes patriotism and valor. The white embodies purity and harmony.

NATIONAL ANTHEM

The national anthem of the Philippines is "Lupang Hinirang", which means Chosen Land.

The anthem tells the story of our love for the Philippines and the bravery of our people. It was first played when we declared independence on June 12, 1898. Singing it shows our pride and reminds us to care for our country.

Let's sing together!

Before the anthem starts, we place our hand over our hearts and face the Philippine flag.

Lupang Hinirang

Bayang magiliw,
Perlas ng silanganan,
Alab ng puso,
sa dibdib mo'y buhay.

Lupang Hinirang,
duyan ka ng magiting.
Sa manlulupig, di ka pasisiil.

Sa dagat at bundok,
sa simoy at sa langit mong bughaw,
May dilag ang tula,
at awit sa paglayang minamahal.

Ang kislap ng watawat mo'y,
tagumpay na nagniningning;
Ang bituin at araw niya,
kailan pa ma'y di magdidilim.

Lupa ng araw ng luwalhati't pagsinta,
buhay ay langit sa piling mo,
Aming ligaya nang pag may mang-aapi,
ang mamatay ng dahil sa iyo.

Chosen Land

Land of the morning,
Child of the sun returning,
With fervor burning,
Thee do our souls adore.

Land dear and holy,
Cradle of noble heroes,
Ne'er shall invaders
Trample thy sacred shore.

Ever within thy skies and through thy clouds
And o'er thy hills and sea,
Do we behold the radiance, feel and throb,
Of glorious liberty.

Thy banner, dear to all our hearts,
Its sun and stars alight,
O never shall its shining field
Be dimmed by tyrant's might!

Beautiful land of love, o land of light,
In thine embrace 'tis rapture to lie,
But it is glory ever, when thou art wronged,
For us, thy sons to suffer and die.

NATIONAL BIRD

Philippine Eagle

The King of the Sky

It is one of the biggest and rarest eagles in the world! With its sharp eyes and strong wings, it soars high above the forest.

It's found only in the Philippines, which makes it a true national treasure!

This mighty bird stands for the strength, bravery, and beauty of the Filipino people.

Let's help protect it and its forest home!

🧠 Fun Fact:

The Philippine Eagle can grow up to 1 meter tall with wings that stretch over 2 meters wide-as wide as a car!

* Photo reference for this drawing is by Aimee Yakas

NATIONAL FLOWER

Sampaguita

The Sampaguita is a small white flower with a soft, sweet smell. It may be tiny, but it stands for purity, honesty, and kindness.

Sampaguita smells wonderful!

Filipinos use it in garlands to welcome guests or as offerings during prayers and special ceremonies.

Fun Fact:

The Sampaguita blooms mostly at night—and each flower lasts only one day, but its scent leaves a lasting memory!

NATIONAL TREE
Narra

It is a tall, sturdy tree that is full of life-just like the Filipino spirit!

It gives cool shade, strong wood for building homes, and even parts that are used in traditional medicine.

In summer, it blooms with bright yellow flowers that light up the forest!

The Narra reminds us to be strong, generous, and full of quiet beauty.

NATIONAL GEM

Philippine Pearl

The Philippine Pearl is a shiny gem found deep in the ocean. It grows inside oysters and takes years to form.

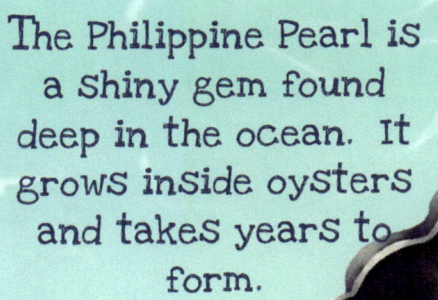

This beautiful gem is called the South Sea Pearl and is known for its soft glow and large size.

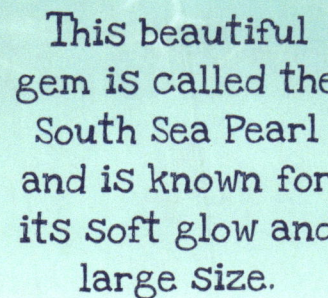

🧠 Fun Fact:

The Philippines has a cool nickname, <u>Pearl of the Orient Seas</u>. This was due to the abundance of natural pearls and the special location of the islands for trade.

CULTURAL SYMBOLS

Mango

Mangoes from the Philippines are among the sweetest in the world! They remind us of the tropical beauty of our country. Whether eaten fresh, dried, or in desserts, mangoes are always a treat.

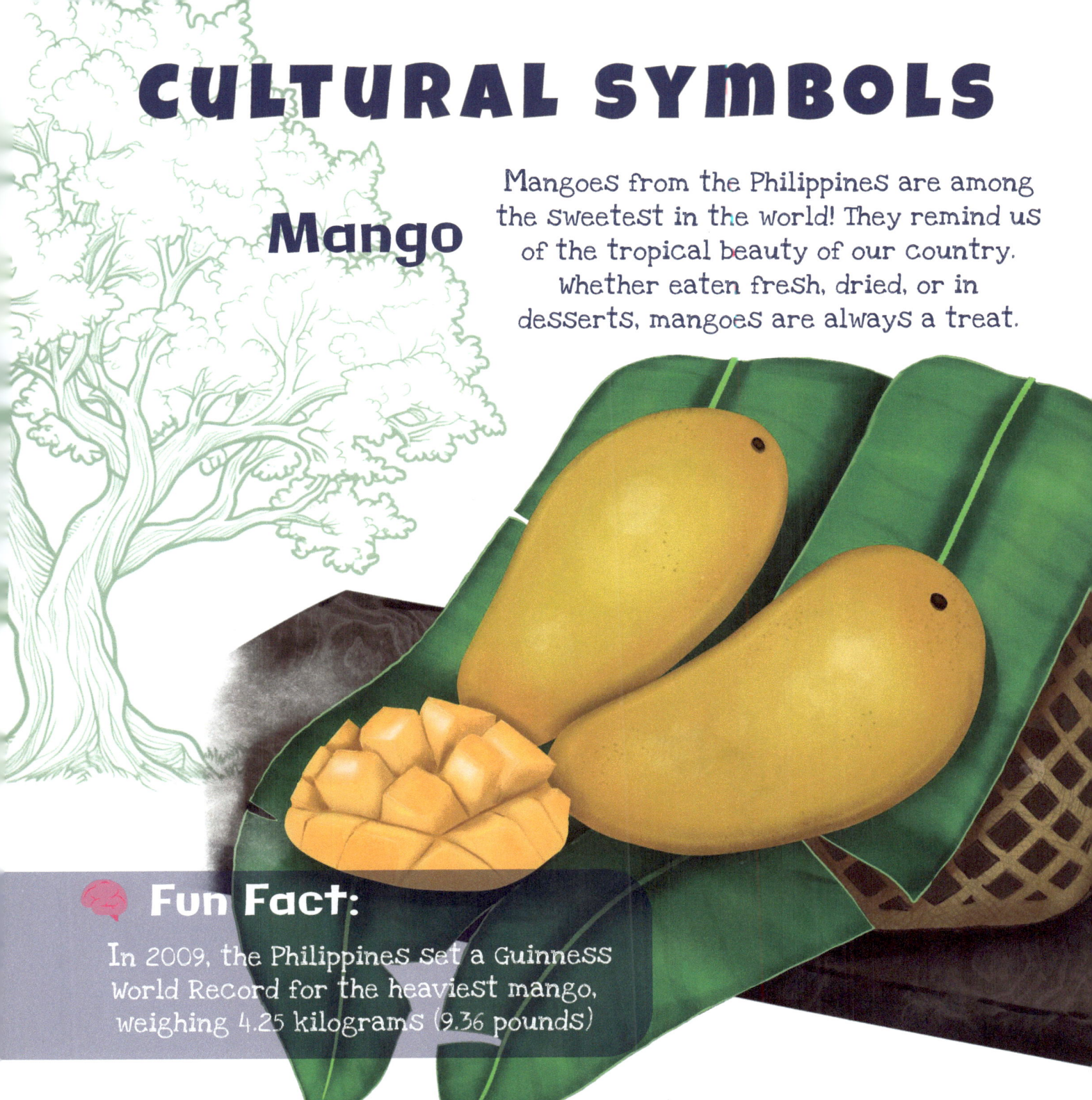

🧠 Fun Fact:

In 2009, the Philippines set a Guinness World Record for the heaviest mango, weighing 4.25 kilograms (9.36 pounds)

Bangus

The bangus (Chanos chanos), or milkfish, is considered the national fish of the Philippines by many Filipinos, although it has not been officially declared as such by law.

Loved for its flavor, it is often cooked in popular dishes like sinigang or fried until crispy. Bangus is also a resilient and adaptable fish, making it easy to farm in various environments such as freshwater, brackish water, and marine waters. Its numerous tiny bones have led to the creation of the popular "boneless bangus," a favorite among Filipinos.

Adobo

Adobo is a favorite food in the Philippines, made with meat marinated in soy sauce, vinegar, garlic, and spices. Each family has its own special recipe, so it's always cooked with love and care.

Jose Rizal

José Rizal used the power of words to awaken the Filipino spirit and inspire the fight for freedom. Through his books and essays, he exposed injustices and ignited the Philippine Revolution. His courage and intellect remind us that true bravery lies in standing up for what is right.

Baro't Saya

The Baro't Saya is a traditional dress that Filipinas wear for celebrations and cultural events. Let's take a closer look at its parts:

Pañuelo (Shawl) - A big, folded scarf worn over the shoulders. It makes the dress look even more elegant and adds a touch of modesty, just like a queen's cape!

Baro (Blouse) - This is a soft, light blouse made from special fabrics like piña or jusi. It has wide, flowy sleeves and pretty embroidery. It's so light that you can almost see through it!

Tapis (Overskirt) - A short, fancy cloth wrapped around the saya. It adds extra beauty and makes the dress even more special!

Saya (Skirt) - A long, beautiful skirt that comes in many colors and patterns. It flows when you walk and makes you feel like a princess!

When girls wear the Baro't Saya, they look graceful and proud—just like the strong and beautiful Filipinas in history!

Barong Tagalog

The Barong Tagalog is a special shirt worn on important days like weddings, graduations, and fiestas. It's light, elegant, and full of history!

Light and Airy - Made from pineapple, silk, or banana fibers, the Barong is a little see-through, keeping you cool in warm weather.

Beautiful Embroidery - The front has hand-stitched patterns of leaves and flowers, making each Barong unique!

Worn Untucked - Unlike other shirts, the Barong is never tucked in! This tradition started during Spanish times.

Comfy and Stylish - Side slits make it easy to move, while long sleeves and fancy cuffs add elegance.

A Symbol of Filipino Pride - More than a shirt, the Barong represents Filipino heritage and tradition.

Bahay Kubo

The Bahay Kubo is more than just a house-it's a symbol of Filipino ingenuity and simple living. Made of bamboo, nipa, and wood, it stays cool in hot weather and blends with nature. Raised on stilts, it protects families from floods while allowing fresh air to flow through. This humble home teaches us the value of resourcefulness, resilience, and living in harmony with the environment-just like our ancestors did.

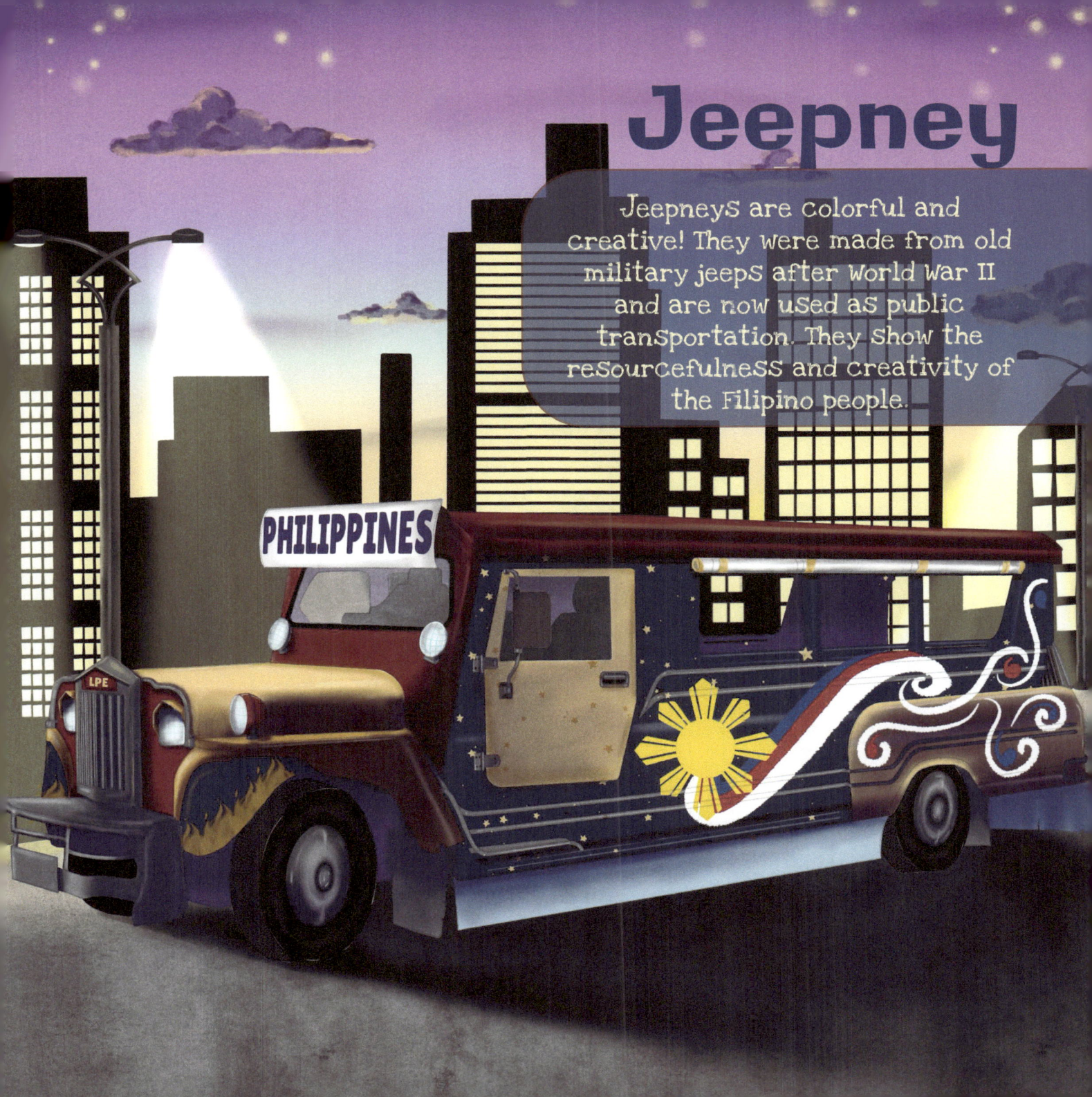

Anahaw

The Anahaw is a big, round, fan-shaped leaf that grows in the Philippines. It's strong, beautiful, and super useful!

People use Anahaw leaves to make fans, hats, roof covers, and decorations, especially during fiestas. In schools and scouting, it's also a symbol of leadership and doing your best.

Carabao

The Gentle Giant of the Fields

The Carabao is strong, calm, and hardworking. It helps farmers plow rice fields and carry heavy loads. More than a helper, it's a symbol of Filipino strength, patience, and determination. This gentle giant reminds us that quiet strength and steady effort can build a better future.

Halo-halo

A Sweet Mix of Filipino Flavors

Halo-Halo means "mix-mix" in Filipino! It's a colorful, icy dessert loved on hot days. Each bowl is different, just like the Philippines-fun, diverse, and full of surprises!

What's Inside Halo-Halo?

- Shaved ice and milk

- Ice cream

- Sweet banana and jackfruit

- Red beans and jelly

- Leche flan or ube on top!

Mix it all together for a taste of Filipino joy in every bite!

Piña Fabric

Did you know you can make cloth from pineapple leaves?  That's how Piña fabric is made! It's light, shiny, and very soft.

This special fabric is often used to make Barong Tagalog and Baro't Saya, especially for weddings and big celebrations.

Making Piña fabric takes a lot of care-each strand is handwoven, making it feel fancy and one-of-a-kind.

It's a beautiful symbol of Filipino creativity and hard work, turning something simple-like pineapple leaves-into something truly elegant!

Pastillas

Pastillas are soft, milky candies made from carabao milk-yum! They're sweet, creamy, and melt in your mouth.

These treats are often made during festivals and family gatherings, especially in Luzon. What makes them extra special? They're wrapped in colorful, hand-decorated paper-just like tiny gifts!

Balete Tree

The Balete tree is one of the most magical trees in the Philippines. With its long, twisting roots and hanging vines, it looks like something straight out of a fairy tale! Many Filipinos believe that this tree is a home for mystical creatures like kapres (giant tree spirits) and dwendes (tiny magical beings). People often show respect to the tree by saying "tabi-tabi po" when passing by, to avoid disturbing the spirits that might live there. Some even make offerings, like food or flowers, to keep the tree's magical residents happy. It's a symbol of the Philippines' rich folklore and spirituality, where every tree and shadow tells a story.

Other Filipino books

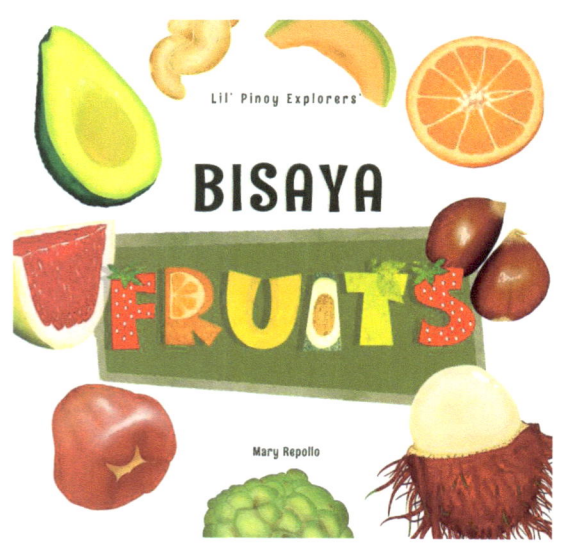

Author's Note

Hi! I'm MARY, a Filipina mom-of-two. I wrote this book for all kids who want to get to know the Philippines, especially migrant kids like mine.

This project of love came from a passing request from my daughter when she expressed her interest in getting to know her cultural roots. It led me down a rabbit hole of internet searches until I decided to create Lil' Pinoy Explorers, with the hope of introducing the Philippines to all children, and build a positive multi-cultural identity as they grow into adulthood.

I hope you enjoy this book together with your kids.

Follow me on Facebook and Instagram at 'Lil' Pinoy Explorers', for kids content related to the Philippines as well as updates on future book releases and giveaways.

Mary Repollo

www.ingramcontent.com/pod-product-compliance
Lightning Source LLC
Chambersburg PA
CBHW041200290426

44109CB00002B/82